THE TAO OF BABIES

for Rose

THE TAO OF BABIES

Illustrated by Chris Riddell

Text by Claire Nielson

Seastone

BERKELEY, CALIFORNIA

Published by: Seastone, an imprint of Ulysses Press
               P.O. Box 3440
               Berkeley, CA 94703
               www.ulyssespress.com

First published in the United Kingdom in 2000 by Ebury Press

Library of Congress Catalog Card Number: 00-107045

ISBN: 1-56975-241-9

Printed in Canada by Transcontinental Printing

10 9 8 7 6 5 4 3 2 1

Cover Design: Leslie Henriques, Sarah Levin
Production staff: David Wells

Distributed in the United States by Publishers Group West
and in Canada by Raincoast Books

CONTENTS

PRINCIPLES

Before follows after

There is an endless current of tireless energy

Outlandish goods ensnare human lives

The source of all things must be understood

Stern and strong are defeated by soft and weak

The softest thing can conquer the strongest

Possessions entail losses

Practice the rituals of the ancestors

Closely observe the processes of creation and evolution

Contemplate the self through the self

Everything easy …

... involves difficulty

The strong remain gentle

Vitality, energy and spirit are not easily sustained

When we walk slowly, we do not stumble

Go higher with every step

RELATIONSHIPS & COMMUNICATIONS

The sound of one's own voice is not
always enjoyed by others

Endeavor to understand that which is alien to you

Understanding others is intelligent ...

... understanding yourself is enlightened

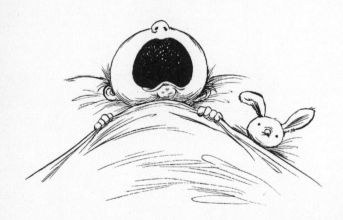

To cry all day without becoming hoarse
indicates complete harmony

Without ever being taught create thousands of things

If violence is inevitable ... be restrained and remain calm

There is great eloquence in silence

We are afraid when we are in favor …

... and when we are not

There can be teaching without words

When no one takes the credit, accomplishment endures

Power over a child is the great illusion

Parents may mistake their desire to talk
for your readiness to listen

Virtuous people do not argue

One can never repay the debt to a mother

SELF-CONTROL

Constant stimulation only distracts

Nothing is harmed if we know when to stop

Anything can be overcome

When we try to control the world we never succeed

Sit calmly in a trance

Pound it and beat it ... it will not last long

What is gripped is lost

Do not prize fine objects and they will not be stolen

Act independently

In the midst of magnificent scenery ...
remain calm and still

Once craving has gone, we see mystery

The wilful lose sight ...

... of the fundamental

WISDOM

Embrace the one and balance the life force

Enlightenment is an understanding of the ordinary

Although we are given names …

... our reality is nameless and mysterious

Look after the belly

Value the teacher

Cultivate emptiness

Learn when to accept the support of others

Reality is as difficult to grasp
as water

The mind is burdened with likes ...

... and dislikes

Avoid hurry ...

... go with the flow

... attain the mysterious profundities

Always aspire to a higher place

Breathe gently

Be older than your ancestors

Be totally sincere

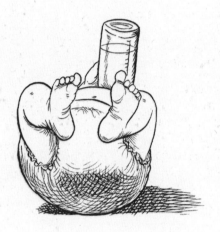

Those who have no desire …

... experience serenity

Sleep soundly ... do not worry through the night